A Special Love

A Book of Poetry

Nedra Anthony

Published and Distributed by:
Professional Publishing House
1425 W. Manchester Ave., Suite B
Los Angeles, California 90047
www.professionalpublishinghouse.com
Drrosie@aol.com
(323) 7503592

Cover Design : Jay De Vance, III
First Printing : August 2013
ISBN: 9780989196048
10987654321
Library of Congress Control Number: 2013913734

DEDICATION

This book is dedicated to my brother Charles Henry Woods who passed away January 21, 2013, at age 73 before I finish writing this book. He was good at helping me realize what he saw in my work. He was my friend, my counselor, my prayer partner, and my critic. I will miss him.

I too, dedicate this book to my sister Lillie Johnetta Hicks, who passed away on April 12, 2013 at the age of 66. Thirteen years ago at the age of 53, Lillie was diagnosed with dementia. By the time, my family and I found there was a problem; Lillie was homeless on the streets of Las Vegas. She came to live with me for seven years. During that time watching someone you love slip away while they are desperately trying to hold on to who they are is breathtaking, but it has made me well aware of how it could have been me. The words I wrote helped me not to allow the circumstance to burn me to get the best of me. Being able to take care of her taught me more than I ever thought I could learn. Her struggle is now over and her mind is perfectly clear. Rest in peace Charles and Lilly, I love you both very much. Thank you for inspiring me to write and finish this book.

ACKNOWLEDGMENTS

I acknowledge God, The Father, who gave me the ability to write every word in this book. To Jesus Christ, The Son of God, who gave His life so I would live long enough to write this book and share it with others, and I acknowledge everyone who has heard of, read or purchased my work. I know there is one poem or another you can relate to about someone you know. I acknowledge everyone who encouraged me, who believed in me, and gave me many things to write about. I acknowledge my Granddaughter, Amber Unique Stevens, who taught me all I needed to know about using a computer. She has brought me more joy than I thought my heart could ever hold, and lastly to Cumire G. Anthony, the man who introduced me to me. Thank you and God bless you.

TABLE OF CONTENTS

A Special Love

A Book of Poetry

The Book

The day I called on the Lord,
doubt filled me up with
guilt and fear.
I prayed with all of my heart
hoping God would hear.

I did whatever I wanted to do
any thought that came to my head.
Not using my best thinking, put me in a place
where I could have ended up dead.

Get all you can while you can
cause when you're dead you're done.
until then I never thought about
when that day would come.

I prayed, "Lord if you can hear me,
my life is in a mess."
No one can help me but you,
please put my fears to rest.

I want to live my life your way
moreover, learn to follow your command.
Work on me, Dear Lord,
until I fit into your plan.

Open my eyes so I can see
how to leave this life behind.
I finally met the one I needed,
I found He was there all the time.

Now, no matter what is going wrong
no matter how things may look,
in the end I know I win
I have read the end of the book.

It Doesn't Cost A Dime

It took many years for me to learn
on Jesus, I could call.
I started each day He gave me
never thinking of Him at all.

My addictions had me bound
they did not fill the void.
not only did it not satisfy,
I saw my life as destroyed.

Fear prevented me from trying,
I had very low selfesteem
because I thought, I would fail,
I was even afraid to dream.

I was drowning in my circumstance,
I did not know how to pray,
even if I had someone to talk to
I did not know what to say.

Someone said I should try Jesus,
the best choice I ever made.
He saved me from certain death,
what a price He paid.

All my sin, fear, and worries
I lay down at His feet,
now His Spirit is my guide,
In Him, I am complete.

I have a new reason for living,
my life will never be the same,
now that I know about Jesus
and the reason that He came.

This is the kind of high
I spent my life trying to find.
Now I do not need a dealer
because it does not cost a dime.

The Greatest Commandment

God sent His Son to die
from heaven up above,
love is the greatest commandment,
all God did, He did with love.

He came to mend the broken hearted
which only He could fix,
to save me from eternal death
and the devils tricks.

He came with the purest love,
to teach me to forgive,
to tell me if I trusted Him,
He could change the way I live.

If I would read and study His word,
learn to follow the path He set,
I could draw even closer to Him,
and put behind me a life of regret.

He said I could make a difference
if I believed His word is true,
if I let His Spirit be my guide
He would show me what to do.

The devils mission is to steal and kill.
He is a robber and a bandit,
our mission is to love each other,
love is the greatest commandment.

He Sends Me

What a mighty God we serve,
He spoke and there was light.
With His mighty power,
He separated day from night.

He separated the sky above
from the earth below,
called all the seas together,
and told them where to flow.

His word moved the waters,
and it drew back from land.
Everything in the universe
Is here by His command.

He made the moon to light the night.
For the day, He made the sun,
Nevertheless, He did not stop there,
more work had to be done.

He made fruit trees and flowers
to replenish He gave them seeds.
It was all a part of His plan,
to fill His creations needs.

In the sea, He put whales and fish.
He made birds to fly through the air,
He called cattle forth from the earth
However, He did not stop there.

He made beast to walk the earth.
He created every living, creeping creature.
Each one after its own kind,
yet still He added a special feature.

Man and woman He created
in the image of Him,
He only gave one command,
left the rest up to them.

As you know, they disobeyed,
did not resist the devils attack.
Jesus Christ had to come
to pay the price to get us back.

When I asked Him to help me
be the best me I could be,
He gave me a willing heart to go
anywhere that He sends me.

Leave Them There

I never thought much of myself,
even thought that I was homely.
Although I had many friends,
inside I was very lonely.

By the time I reached age twelve,
drugs had me strung.
I got high every day,
everyone I knew was thugs.

Even though I was still a child,
a sober day was very rare.
I carried many burdens,
I needed help to bear.

At age forty sitting on a bench
in the park across the street,
I started to cry, I do not know why,
seemed life's problems had me beat.

I do not know how long I cried,
but when I finally ran out of tears
I felt a peace inside of me,
I had not felt for years.

Suddenly a woman sat down beside me,
where she came from, I did not see.

She said, "My child, I have been sent
to tell you, that you are free.

Tell the Lord that you believe,
that He rose from the dead,
that he is the Son of God.
I repeated the words she said.

From today until forever,
you are in His loving care.
She smiled and said, "Jesus loves you,
give Him your cares and leave them there."

Running Out of Time

Jesus reveals His love through us
when we show His love to others.
He said constantly pray,
for all your sisters and brothers.

When you share with someone
how He has changed your life,
about how He died on the cross,
to pay the ultimate price.

How His word has a calming effect,
when your heart is full of fear,
that He will never leave you,
that He is always near.

Tell how His word renews your mind
each time you read,
how His Word builds your confidence
to believe you will succeed.

Tell about those weary days
you had to fight to do His will,
how He loves you so much,
there is no need He will not fill.

If you talk, people will listen
to every word you have to say.
God has opened the door for you
do not let this chance slip away.

Our time is getting shorter,
we must all keep this in mind.
there are many souls out there,
who is running out of time.

Glory In The Cross

Dear God make me a mansion,
in which you want to live.
Fill my heart with compassion
that is always willing to give.

Help me seek your kingdom first,
not seek the wisdom of man.
Help me to follow the path you set,
as closely as I can.

Help me be more like Jesus,
trusting in His Holy name.
Prepare me to walk in victory,
from sin help me refrain.

Teach me to walk by faith,
and never to walk by sight.
Help me stop doing wrong,
when I know what is right.

Fill my heart with the desire
to walk closer every day.
Give me the courage I will need
to come back when I go astray.

From my heart I give, you praise
for all you have already done.
Help me see the glory in the cross
that Jesus Christ died on.

Up To Me

The blood of an over comer
is running through my veins,
since I accepted Jesus Christ,
my life has not been the same.

He cleared my vision so I could see
the wrong in what I was doing,
showed me my life could change,
if His kingdom I was pursuing.

I can only live one day at a time
once I faced that fact,
He gave me the courage to carry on
with no desire to ever turn back.

I had to stop seeing myself
through the eyes of my past.
His Spirit helped me understand
God's word I can grasp.

In prayer, my heart is prepared,
when sin comes, I can resist.
I have stopped going to Him
with my usual, "I want list."

Now when life's storm do come,
I know how to be quiet and still.
He is teaching me through His word
how to walk in His will.

Nothing I've ever done or thought,
will ever be able to compare
to the love Jesus Christ revealed,
when my sins he came to bear.

Even when I stumble and fall,
or those times I go astray,
if I call, Him He will answer,
but! It is up to me to pray.

The Foot of The Cross

For years I have been searching
with a desire to understand,
why the God of all creation,
fit me into His plan.

Everything that He is
Within and of Himself,
I found so hard to believe
there was a way I could help.

He said to have faith in His Son,
read each word He has spoken,
He would be with me in battle,
sins power would be broken.

He told me of His love for me,
on His love I could rely,
it was His choice to become a man
and the reason He had to die.

He said if you walk away from the world
to follow the plans I have for you,
there are no limits to the heights,
I will take you to.

I gave my life so you could live.
I did it all to save your soul.
Without me, you can do nothing,
your life, I want control.

There is no power on this earth
that can ever take you from my hand.
Read and study my word,
it will help you understand.

Go and share this good news
with those you know are lost.
Tell them the pathway to heaven,
begins at the foot of the cross.

Nedra Anthony ❦ 28

The Answer Man

On a clear day, I see the mountains,
each has a snowcovered top.
I thought, "How can anyone not believe,
God gave us all we've got."

He gave us breath to breathe.
He gave us hearing and sight,
the ability to touch and taste,
Most importantly, He gave us the light.

He gave us the sun and moon,
clouds to bring spring showers.
He gave us a nose to smell,
food, cooking and all the flowers.

He gave us bodies to live in,
a spirit and a soul.
He gave us the Holy Spirit,
so our life he could shape and mold.

He gave us the right to choose,
to walk in all His freedom.
He gave His word to teach us,
how we could seek his kingdom.

He gave us hearts to love,
no need to live in defeat.
He gave us joy to get us through
when times are not so sweet.

Still we have these questions
we are afraid to ask.
We hold on to our fears,
while clinging to our past.

Some say you will not make it,
Jesus says yes you can.
Come to Him with your questions,
Jesus is the answer man.

Amazing Grace

Going to work each morning
I see the homeless on the street,
Living in cardboard boxes,
searching through trash for something to eat.

It is a minutebyminute struggle,
having to beg to stay alive.
On cold and rainy nights
some have failed to survive.

I do not know what put them there,
I did not even try to understand,
I would just pass them by
when I could lend a helping hand.

I thought, "Why don't they get a job?"
I kept looking until I found mine.
I thought about how long it took
to be hired just part time.

The next day I was caught at the light,
a woman who looked very strange
knocked on my window and asked
if I could spare any change.

I did not have any change,
the smallest I had was a five.
I gave it to her and she began to sing,
"thank you Lord, I am still alive."

She said, "I know The Lord sent you,"
for anyone to help is very rare.
I thank you for the money, but
I need a whole lot of prayer."

As I drove away, I began to pray
for that woman on the corner.
I knew that it was possible
one day I could join her.

God used her to bless me,
put a big smile on her face.
Even in the little things,
I can see His amazing grace.

Everything To Gain

I humbled myself and went to
the Father with my petition.
The Holy Spirit helped me see,
how to change my current condition.

I told Him about my temptation,
I asked Him to give me strength
not to stray away from the path,
help me use to my common sense.

The enemy knows my weaknesses,
It is his mission to keep me weak.
He knows I am no longer his
It is Gods kingdom that I seek.

While seeking Him I found Him,
my salvation I have received.
I am now a child of God
from the moment I believed.

None of my fears came from God,
power and love is what he gave.
His word came alive in my heart,
there is no doubt my soul is saved.

When I gave my life to Christ,
I gave Him every hurt and pain.
I knew I had nothing to lose,
but everything to gain.

Nedra Anthony ❦ 34

Let It Shine

When God gave all power to Jesus,
Jesus gave the power to me.
I could choose to live in bondage
or live a life that made me free.

When I called upon His name
He immediately came to help.
I was sick of being tired
and I could not help myself,

but when he came into my life
he really turned my life around.
He picked me up out of the pit and
Put my feet on solid ground.

As I began to read His Word
to find out what he had said,
His spirit helped me understand
the scriptures that I read.

The more I read the more I learned
about what he has done for me.
If I follow the path, he has set
I could walk in victory.

Now when I get down on my knees,
to The Lord I pray.
I thank Him for small bits of joy
He gives to me each day.

He made my life more productive,
through His Word, he renews my mind.
He is filling me with his light
and I want to let it shine.

Hope

God the Father is almighty,
He is worthy of all the praise.
He sent his son to fulfill the law,
who, from death, he was raised.

He made the way for me to know,
I am no longer condemned.
He came for me because
I could not get to Him.

He said he would be with me
if I am low or flying high.
His love would last forever,
on that love, I could rely.

His love, His spirit and His Word
will help me follow his plan.
He gave me what I needed to learn,
every one of His commands.

He gave me understanding
through thought, hearing, and sight,
to learn to walk in His love
now I can get it right.

No words I could utter
would be able to express,
the newness of life I experienced
through God's grace and holiness.

So, when life's problems get me down
and feel I cannot cope.
I reach beyond my problem by faith,
this is the substance of my hope.

My Savior My Lord, My King

On the day Jesus Christ was born
the Eastern Star shone bright
to let the whole world know
the savior was born that night.

He chose to become a man
so my soul would not be lost.
It was not easy but worth it,
He came to go to the cross.

He was sent to assure me of
the love he wanted to give,
said if I believed in Him
He would change the way I live.

If you walk away from the world
and live your life my way,
believe I am who I said I am,
It will keep you from going astray.

I found out how much he loves me,
He would forgive me for all my sin.
I opened the door to my heart,
He willing entered in.

It was on that day I understood
On Him, I could cast my care,
when I called on His name
He was right there.

Now each day I celebrate
the love he came to bring.
I know in my heart without a doubt
He is My Savoir, My Lord, and My King.

First

When life's troubles overwhelmed me
I tried to move much faster.
After running all over the place
I finally went to the master.

There are times words do not come
when my heart is filled with despair,
sometimes I must remind myself
that God is always there.

I tried to work things out my way,
did my best to stay in control,
But because of my lack of faith,
I never reached my goal.

I should have gone to The Lord
when all my problems began,
instead, I used my own strength
now the walls were closing in.

When finally I called on Him,
everything was falling apart.
I just needed to face the fact,
that I was not so smart.

It seemed everything I tried,
only made matters worse.
I could have saved myself a lot of time,
had gotten on my knees first.

Nedra Anthony ❦ 42

Jesus Christ Is Lord

Every day of life is a miracle,
blessed are we to breathe God's breath.
Sometimes he seems so far away, but
remember He has never left.

Man gave away what God gave,
so sad on man, He could not rely.
so, He prepared a tree on Calvary,
on which our savior would die.

He was tried and convicted,
crucified on a cross.
Although he died, and rose again,
He came back after paying the cost.

He lived His life free from sin,
knowing his body was a temple
showing us it could be done.
Christ did all he could to make it simple.

He wants us to walk in the fullness
of what we were created for.
none of us has ever known,
a love like this before.

The more we learn about Him
the clearer we can see,
with Him, nothing is impossible,
we can be who he wants us to be.

Without faith, we cannot please Him.
He has helped us understand,
it is not an easy road to walk,
but His word say's that we can.

So, we press toward the mark,
strive with Him on one accord.
We all know within our hearts
That Jesus Christ is Lord.

Nedra Anthony ❦ 44

The Man

A long time ago, there was a man
who loved each one of us, so
He devised an eternal plan,
that he came to let us know.

This man came and lived among us,
left his home from above.
He lived a sinless life before us,
with no boundaries to His love.

For our sake, He endured temptation,
He overcame all that is wrong.
He would heal the fearful heart,
showing in Him, we can be strong.

He would hang on a wooden cross,
with no chance of acquittal.
Evil would try to conquer good,
this man would be in the middle.

His life would change many lives
for anyone who called his name.
Some will walk away from Him,
not wanting their lives to change.

Some of those who will not believe
the victory for us was won,
by the man who fought the battle,
God's only begotten son.

We can give Him all of our burdens,
for He made the pathway clear.
Now we can talk directly to God,
pray in His name and god will hear.

He is waiting to hear them say,
I place my life into your hand.
When they do, they will know
Jesus Christ is the man.

True Reflection

In the world the more I wanted
the less I seem to get,
but in Christ I am complete,
my every need is met.

Jesus is my Lord and Savior
He is my righteousness.
Since I gave my life to Him
I have been truly blessed.

In my life was only confusion,
everything was going wrong.
I learned it is in my weakness
that He will make me strong.

I found out that he died
Therefore, I could be set free.
the decision was made
before God created the tree.

He conquered hell and death,
then he rose from the grave.
The blood he shed was for me,
now my soul is saved.

God's power and love is shown
by His resurrection.
He lived, He died, and He lived again.
He is God's true reflection.

That Moment

If I knew then what I know now
when I thought I knew it all.
I would have listened to advice
to heed the Saviors' call.

When I finally heard Him,
I was broken and undone.
He had been calling me for years
but, I refused to come.

The storms of life surrounded me,
my heart was filled with sorrow.
I was drowning in my circumstance,
with little hope for tomorrow.

I did not know which way to turn,
wondered how I got to this place.
when something inside of me said,
"There are facts that you must face."

You see you cannot make it alone,
try counting the times you have tried.
Think about what you were taught,
for your sake, Jesus Christ died.

I remembered what my mother said
before I moved out on my own.
"Jesus will never leave you,"
You will never be alone."

He stands at your hearts door,
just let Him take control.
You must know within your heart
that He died to save your soul.

I went to Him with a thankful heart.
I thanked the father for the son.
My life has not been the same
from that moment on.

Nedra Anthony ❦ 50

In His Hands

I have risen above my circumstance
because Jesus has set me free.
I can soar like the eagle,
and not be moved by the storms I see.

I told the world I believed.
He then filled me with His Spirit,
set me free from the law.
He gave His life to fulfill it.

He gave me the faith to believe
if I want to change, I can.
He gave his word to renew my mind,
He made me fit into His plan.

He pointed me in the right direction,
showing me how to follow His lead.
He has given my heart assurance,
there is no doubt I will succeed.

Now that I believe, it was His blood
that cleansed me from my sin,
my eyes are now open, I could see,
knowing when the battle is over I win.

So now when storms are coming,
I find myself running for cover.
I run into my Savior's arms,
Knowing it will soon blow over.

All of my faith is in Jesus,
it is all a part of His plans.
He knows that I know,
my life is in His hands.

Special Love

My mother dear is no longer here,
with all my heart, I still miss her.
I miss the times we used to talk,
it was then I could hug and kiss her.

She had a heart full on love,
all children were her kids.
She lived her life caring for others,
consider herself, she never did.

At age sixteen, I got pregnant.
This is what my mother said,
"If the child is yours, it is mine,
now take yourself to bed."

After my daughter was born
I became very sick.
My heart stopped, my veins collapsed,
but my dear mother never missed a trick.

She sat down beside my bed
never ceasing to smile,
praying Lord let your will be done.
Won't you please spare my child.

She took me to God in prayer,
she would always do that first.
I now stand before you today,
you see how well her plan worked.

Sometimes when I look in the mirror
I see her looking back at me,
asking, "Nedra are you being
who God created you to be?"

I keep asking myself that question,
while reflecting on my past.
I wish that I could tell her
that my answer would be yes.

She left here twentyeight years ago,
she is at home with God above.
I thank Him for letting me share
a very special love.

Nedra Anthony ❦ 54

I'm Losing My Sister

When is the dance Val?
Is what my sister would say,
having already forgotten,
the dance was yesterday.

Dementia is stealing my sister,
I wonder at times if she is still there.
On Tuesday's when we are together,
I bathe her and do her hair.

She might ask, "Where is Ricky?"
Her only son. I remind her
he is away for a while,
as soon as he can, he will come.

We can be sitting in the same room,
yet sometimes she is hard to find.
I keep on looking for her
using whatever comes to mind.

One thing made a little difference,
It was a pill called Aricept.
I saw a change here and there,
but it never really seemed to help.

I watched her slip away,
praying her memory would last,
but she can't remember very much
when we talk about our past.

Memory lane is a oneway street,
getting harder for her to travel.
It hurts me deep in my heart
to see her everyday unravel.

I try nostalgia, mementoes,
and memories to help her reminisce.
She remembers for only a moment,
then soon she will forget.

It's Tuesday again, I pick her up,
as I always do.
She sees me and her big smile says,
"Oh yeah, I remember you."

We talk for a while and
have a good laugh.
I give her a cap full of Hennessey
to get her to take a bath,

I show her love, I give her a hug,
and each time we part I kiss her.
I do everything I know to do
to hold on to my sister.

I cherish moments I spend with her,
and sometimes ask, "Lord how can this be?"
In my heart and mind, I fear the day,
she may not remember me.

I Can't Remember

Just a line to say I am living,
I am not among the dead.
Though I'm getting more forgetful,
and mixed up in the head.

I got used to my arthritis.
To my dentures, I am resigned.
I can manage my bifocals,
but! God I miss my mind.

Sometimes, I can't remember
when I stand at the foot of the stairs,
if I must go up for something,
or did I just come down from there?

Before the fridge so often
my poor mind filled with doubt,
did I just put some food away or
did I come to take something out.

There I am in the dark,
my nightcap on my head.
I don't know if I am retiring for the night,
or if I just got out of bed.

Nedra Anthony ❦ 58

Is it my turn to write you?
I don't know, but no need to keep score.
I may think I have already written,
and I just don't want to be a bore.

So remember that I love you,
and wish that you were near,
now it is nearly mail time,
and I must say good bye, my dear.

Here I stand beside the mailbox,
with my face so very red.
Instead of mailing you my letter,
I have opened it instead.

God Sent His Love

The secret of life is letting go
of anything, that holds me back.
Something in my life had to change,
I have finally face that fact.

I would never ever be satisfied,
trying to fill my own cup.
Things I was pouring into it
were the things I needed to give up.

Hangups, hobbies and habits,
had me broken and undone.
With little hope for a tomorrow,
I still hoped that it would come.

I treated myself so bad.
I now know I needed help.
I looked for love in wrong places
trying to find it by myself.

That is when I heard about Jesus
who gave to all a measure of faith.
I found out he died to save my soul
and my sins would be erased.

Nedra Anthony ❦ *60*

Not knowing I walked in darkness
I was so blind I could not see.
God sent His love with Jesus,
and Jesus came to bring it to me.

Not A Destination

As women we work harder
to make it in this life.
We have many roles to play,
mother, daughter, friend and wife.

We are doctors, lawyers, and teachers,
businesswomen, artist and poets.
We are sure of who we are and
we want the world to know it.

We have many professions,
too numerous to mention.
We are moving ahead,
gaining more attention.

We have to struggle,
to come up with a plan.
Always trusting in The Lord,
never letting go of His hand.

It is He, who helps us see
woman is an institution, and
more of us, everyday
are finding our solution.

Nedra Anthony ⚘ 62

Sister encouraging sister,
working together as a team.
One sister helping another
to realize her dream.

Through it all we have learned
by error, trials and inspiration.
Success is a journey,
not a destination.

You Knew

Father you know everything.
You knew what I would become.
You knew the second I would believe,
in the love you sent by your son.

You knew the minute I would see,
how much I needed your love
to overcome sin in my life.
For my life, you had a cause.

You knew the hour and circumstance
when on you I would call.
You knew the trials I would face and
how many times I would fall.

You knew the day I would realize
without you, I was lost.
The week I would deny myself
moreover, took up my own cross.

You knew within my heart,
I longed to find my purpose.
You knew I followed your Spirit's lead,
to bring my purpose to the surface.

Nedra Anthony ❦ 64

You knew these words would be written,
all who heard them would be amazed,
knowing they too came from you,
giving you all the praise.

You knew I would learn to trust you,
as my faith grew and grew.
Every day you are showing me,
that all the time you knew.

Your Will Be Done

I told myself I trusted God,
nevertheless, my actions showed I lied.
I could not make my actions valid,
no matter how hard I tried.

I prayed, "Dear God in heaven,
I sure hope you hear my prayer."
I am going to church this Sunday,
I want to see you there.

You said to come just as I am,
even if, in misery and strife.
I want to meet the man
who died to save my life.

Give me the courage I need to face
the challenge of being myself.
I am aware I cannot do it alone,
I will surely need some help.

Open my eyes so I can see.
Please open my ears to hear.
Help me believe within my heart
I have no need to fear.

Nedra Anthony ❦ 66

Take anything that hinders me from
drawing closer to you each day.
give me the heart and mind
to come boldly to your throne when I pray

I pray my prayers reach your ears.
Thank you for letting me come.
If you hear me send the answer,
in my life let your will be done.

My Eyes On You

Thank you Lord for giving me
a new life so I could live.
Thank you for guiding my footsteps.
with a heart that is willing to give.

I am amazed I lived so long
without you in my life.
Troubles could have been avoided,
that cut like a knife.

Thank you for watching over me
when those troubles came my way,
for hearing my hearts prayers
when I had no words to say.

Knowing you heard me,
opened my eyes to see
how you wanted to change my life,
you were only waiting for me.

You are helping me fight my battles.
Your Spirit helps me to dominate,
the other side of me I have grown to hate.

Thank for what you have yet to do.
Thank you for all you have done.

Nedra Anthony ❦ *68*

Thank you for loving me so much
that you sent your son.

Thank you for helping me to see
you are with me as I go through,
helping me face my problems
while keeping my eyes on you.

Invite Him In

I spent years running from God,
but as time passed I began to slow down.
In spite of all my running,
I was not gaining any ground.

Addictions, doubts, guilt and fears,
grew worse with each day that passed.
I had no place to run or hide,
I did not think I would last.

When I found a place to lay my head
I remembered what Mama used to say,
"Before you go to sleep each night,
always take the time to pray."

God brought you through another day.
You should give Him a minute or two.
All night long, he is there,
just watching over you."

He chose you before you were born,
to walk in his loving care.
You can call Him any time,
even if you think, he is not there.

Nedra Anthony ❦ 70

I was a servant to the Devil's will,
He did not want to let me go.
He ask if he could keep me, but
God in his mercy told Him no.

God already made the way,
to set me free from sin.
He was patiently waiting
for me to invite Him in.

He Can't Have Me

I thank God for choosing me.
He has made me well aware,
The world has no love for me,
I would be dead if I' had stayed there.

When I heard Jesus call my name,
I was lying flat on my back.
He allowed me to hear Him,
knowing my life was way off track.

It was then I was told a story
about a man from Galilee,
who gave his life on the cross
to show his love for me.

He knew each time I had sinned,
yet he loved me anyway.
I learned I did not have to listen
to what the Devil had to say.

The Devil thinks I still belong to Him,
but he better think again.
Jesus has already fought the battle,
He has chosen to be my friend.

Nedra Anthony ❦ 72

As I learn to let go and let God,
I learn to do His will his way.
I am becoming an over comer
by trusting Him each time I pray.

There is nothing the Devil can do to me,
though I am under constant attack.
I know he will not stop trying but,
Jesus will not let Him have me back.

Praise

Meeting Jesus changed my life,
His Spirit came to live in me.
My eyes are open, now I can see
how fruitful my life could be.

I told Him I would stop trying
to make Him fit into my mold
then I asked Him to come in,
to be the Savior of my soul.

I was locked in constant battle,
did wrong knowing to do right.
I was never prepared for battle,
I did not even know how to fight.

It took me almost forty years
to finally reach my bottom,
now I shake my head and wonder,
how I ever lived without Him.

He took away that part of me
that did not want to believe.
Everything His Word said
I would be able to achieve.

Nedra Anthony ❦ 74

Jesus took the life I lived and
turned it upside down.
He did not stop until I could me see
he was turning my life around.

I learned to trust Him day by day,
that in the love he came to give.
I wanted my life to reflect
I am completely His.

Now no matter what the situation
or whatever I must go through,
I lift my voice and praise Him,
because praise is what I do.

Learn How To Pray

Because of the love of God
my life is anew.
Meeting Him has changed my life,
He also changed my point of view.

He told me I could be saved,
but it must be my own decision.
He would show me the way
to receive all of His provisions.

New birth is a gift,
meant to cleanse the heart.
He died and rose again,
to give me a brand new start.

He knew well before I did,
this day would come.
He knows more about me than I do.
He knows everything I have done.

I took myself through many changes,
my life was going downhill.
In my despair, I met Jesus Christ.
I found out His love is real.

Nedra Anthony 🌹 *76*

Jesus gave me living water,
gave me sense enough to of it, drink.
Sometimes it blows my mind,
the way I used to think.

Today I am still struggling,
trying to live my life God's way.
I am doing a whole lot better,
since I learned how to pray.

He Is Faithful

Way back when I knew it all,
I moved out on my own.
I left all that love and comfort
because I thought, I was grown.

Things went well for a while
until all my bills came due,
Mama said,
"There would be days like this.
I bit off more than I could chew."

I tried until I could try no more
until finally I concluded;
I had tried everything,
but prayer was not included.

No amount of my own strength
could help me make it in this life.
Alone I could not meet the challenge,
I had to call on Jesus Christ.

I asked if he would walk with me.
I asked Him to be my friend,
to lead me down the crooked roads,
I knew would sometimes bend.

Nedra Anthony ❦ 78

God is with me wherever I go,
helping me to understand
He will never leave me alone.
I must hold on to his hand.

God saved me from myself.
I am forever grateful.
No matter what the challenge
I know that he is faithful.

He Has Risen

Jesus came to fulfill the law,
with no chance of being acquitted.
He was tried and convicted
of crimes, he never committed.

He stood there before Pilate,
who found no fault in Him.
He gave His life on the cross,
so I would not be condemned.

God knew what had to be done,
He came to pave the way
allowing Him to be crucified
was the price he chose to pay.

The people screamed crucify Him!
We want this man to die!
Many of them did not even know,
they were convinced of a lie.

On the cross Jesus experienced
the ultimate kind of grief.
His Father turned His back on Him,
then His Spirit he released.

Nedra Anthony ❦ 80

In the middle of the day was darkness,
with thunder, lighting and rain.
Jesus had fulfilled His mission,
It was the reason that he came.

His body was taken off the cross,
put in a tomb covered by a stone.
Jesus Christ would rise again,
but the hope of the people was gone.

When Mary approached the tomb,
she saw the stone rolled aside.
Her eyes filled with tears,
as she walked closer, she cried.

She left and returned again,
to where Christ's body was laid.
Angels told her not to cry,
He is no longer in the grave.

Jesus Christ had won the battle,
when His life he laid it down.
He conquered hell, death could not
keep Him in the ground.

He Was There

Accepting Jesus changed my life.
Trusting Him has made me free,
now that my eyes are opened,
I can clearly see.

I must learn to be prepared,
each day will bring a fight
against that other me
who wants to do wrong, not right.

Once I understood that fact
God came to save my soul.
I was also able to see
He would not fit into my mold.

The Holy Spirit is teaching me
All I need to know, and
With each lesson I am learning
how my faith can grow and grow.

Through His Word, I can know Him,
Learn to follow his command.
So, when life's storms come upon me,
I will know how to stand.

Nedra Anthony ❦ *82*

My search is finally over.
I found what I sought to find.
I had been searching for a Savior
Jesus Christ was there all the time.

He Is There

Elohim is almighty God,
He is the multibreasted one.
He gives life to everything
under and beyond the sun.

God is Alpha and Omega,
He has always been.
He is Jehovah God forever,
the beginning and the end.

God is Adonai
in complete control.
He knows what is going on
in the life of every soul.

El Shadi is allsufficient,
every need he will meet.
Be it food on your table,
or shoes on your feet.

If there is trouble in your mind or body,
affecting how you think or feel,
there is no sickness or disease
Jehovah Rapha cannot heal.

Nedra Anthony ❦ 84

In Him there is no shadow of turning,
on Him you can rely.
He is Jehovah Kadash,
the only God who can satisfy.

He provided the clouds for the day,
for the night the pillar of fire.
What is needed is provided,
He is Jehovah Jireh.

We must always follow His lead,
in a prayerful manner.
He goes before us in battle,
Jehovah Nissi is our banner.

When the battle is over
all fears shall be released.
He is Jehovah Shalom,
God who gives us peace.

He is a loving God and Father,
on Him, we can cast our cares.
No matter where you are, just
call on His name and He is there.

I Still Hear

I thank my Lord everyday
for leaving His home above.
I remember Mama said,
"He is the God of love."

Even before, I knew Him
He came to set me free.
I remember Mama saying,
"His love included me."

I did not even know Him, but
with my back against the wall,
I remember Mama saying,
"All I had to do was call."

I really needed to talk to God,
but I did not know what to say.
I remember Mama called and said,
"Let's take this time to pray."

I began to cry as Mama prayed,
"Lord keep her in your care."
Show her how much you love her
and that you are always there."

Nedra Anthony ❦ 86

Take away her doubts and fears,
let your work in her begin.
Help her to see and know
you are a real true friend.

God let her live to see me saved.
Three years later, he took her home.
I remember Mama said,
"He will never leave you alone."

At times I look in the mirror,
and the longer I look I can see,
the image of my Mama
smiling back at me.

Twentyeight years have gone by,
seems like only yesterday.
She is living in her own mansion,
yet I can still hear Mama pray.

The Love

My life was in a whirlwind,
sin kept me burdened with its demands
until I met my Savior
who plucked me from sins hands.

Sin always took me further
than I ever wanted to go.
In my mind, I wanted to stop.
Why I kept going back, I do not know.

Once I got where I was going,
I stayed longer than I wanted to stay
it cost me a whole lot more
than I ever intended to pay.

I finally hit rock bottom,
my body racked with pain,
there was only oneway to turn,
so, I called on Jesus name.

Day by day as I learn His Word,
the clearer I am able to see.
It was His choice to let me live,
not let me die in my misery.

Nedra Anthony ❦ 88

He has a purpose for my life.
He won the battle for my soul.
He was only waiting for me
to let Him take control.

Without God, I was going nowhere.
When my life took a different turn,
I found out he would freely give
the love I was trying to earn.

Enough Love

God is a big God.
He is everywhere.
There is no place I could run
where he would not be there.

God is a gracious God.
There is beauty in His grace.
God cared so much for me,
He chose to die in my place.

God is a merciful God.
He is with me through all my pain.
I thought my life was over
until I was born again.

As soon as I called out to Him
my eyes filled with tears.
I knew that he had heard me,
when I confessed my sins and fears.

I thanked Him for not giving up on me,
and for watching over me as I ran.
I asked Him to change my direction
and help me to follow his plan.

Nedra Anthony ❦ 90

I know He is the God of love,
on that love, I can rely.
I have been trying to earn it,
though foolish for me to try.

He showed the greatness of His love
by sending His son.
He is the almighty God,
with enough love for everyone.

Your Source

Sometimes it blows me away,
the excuses I can invent
to do just what I want to do,
not exercising my common sense.

I drove right over what was right.
I knew I was going wrong.
Headed back to my old life,
thinking this time, I would be strong.

I leaned to my own understanding,
which I knew I should not do.
Fear had tightened its grip,
in time, my deed was through.

But God in His tender mercy,
took away all of my despair.
He forgave me when I turned
to Him in prayer.

God said, "Go your way and sin no more,"
then He filled my heart with peace.
Read The Word to find direction,
your faith you can increase.

Nedra Anthony ❧ 92

Go share what I have done for you
not one soul do I want to lose.
Tell people my love has no limits,
all their sins I shall remove.

You must be aware of your enemy
who seeks only to devour
follow my Spirit and listen to Him,
He is your source of power.

Keep It Burning

Way back when I knew it all
I moved out on my own.
I left love and comforts of home
because I thought, I was grown.

For many years after I grew up
I started doing my own thing.
I was not seeking The Lord
or the joy His love could bring.

I always knew what I had to do
to reach my higher calling,
by living life my way,
I kept constantly falling.

We went to church when the doors were open,
not going meant, we had no way.
My mother's wisdom, love and prayers
is the reason I am here today.

Call His name, He will hear you,
is what my mother always said.
Now I can see her wisdom and
why she drummed it in my head.

Nedra Anthony ❦ *94*

I made it through storms in my life,
God used them all to help me see.
He was waiting for me to decide,
to truly want to be free.

As I learn more about The Lord,
I stopped doing things I used to do.
With His Word shut in my bones,
I am here to share it with you.

Today I look back over the years
at where he has brought me from.
I leaned not to my understanding,
no matter what trials may come.

Brothers and sister if you trust Him,
in your heart, He will put a yearning.
He will give you a lamp filled with oil,
it is up to you to keep it burning.

A Better Day

Troubles rained down on me,
storm winds were blowing hard.
I did not have on the belt of truth,
and I got caught off guard.

Prepared for battle, I was not.
I thought the fight would blow over.
Without my breastplate of righteousness
I found myself running for cover.

Troubles kept coming,
Storms were hostile.
I realized I left at home,
the peace that is the gospel.

The enemy had me cornered.
He was not wasting any time,
I could not put out the fiery darts,
my shield of faith I left behind.

I ran off and forgot my helmet,
no salvation to cover my head.
My mind was in total confusion,
my heart filled with dread.

Nedra Anthony ❦ 96

I also left the sword of the Spirit,
but in my car on the way to work,
I thought of all Jesus did for me
and I felt just like a jerk.

I turned around and went back home,
fell on my knees to pray,
I put on the armor of God
and looked ahead to a better day.

Best For Me

God is the God of love,
His love is so undeserved.
He created me to glorify Him,
to depend upon His Word.

When I believed His Word is true
His plan began to unfold.
His love for me is so deep,
He died to save my soul.

He gave me a willing heart,
with a desire to seek his face.
He gave His Spirit to guide me.
He gave His mercy and grace.

I am learning as I read,
to live life as I should live,
and be willing to receive
everything He has to give.

He left the choice up to me.
I am so glad He let me choose.
I asked Him to mold and shape me
into a vessel that he could use.

Nedra Anthony ❦ 98

I believe with all of my heart,
there is no need He cannot fill.
I want to spend my time wisely,
I want to practice doing his will.

In Him all things are possible.
His Spirit has helped me see,
by trusting Him I will find
whatever He does is best for me.

His Crown

When life's storms come upon me,
I do all I know to do.
In my heart, I am sure
God will see me through.

I have fought many battles,
I am on the destroyers list.
When two of us will agree,
Jesus Christ is in our mist.

He is always with me,
when I go through fiery trials.
He prepares me with the truth
to stand against the devils wiles.

Test comes hard and heavy.
What to do was decided.
When Jesus died on the cross,
all I needed for my life was provided.

The day I took Him at His Word,
I was born again.
my past washed away in His blood,
even allfuture sin.

He is the way, the truth, and the life.
He died to save my soul,
He paid the ultimate price,
Now He is in complete control.

I love Him for all He has done.
He laid His life down,
then picked it up again,
so I could wear His crown.

A Place To Grow

For twentyfive years, I went to church.
Sunday was always my favorite day,
it was when I praised The Lord,
and bowed my head while others prayed.

I was convinced I knew The Lord
in a very special way.
Seldom did I talk to Him,
because I did not know what to say.

Still I thought I had it going on,
thought I had a Christ like mind.
I did not pray the rest of the week,
I could never find the time.

My confidence began to waiver,
sometimes I walked in fear.
I said, "Speak to me Lord this Sunday,
tell me what I need to hear."

As I drove past a building, I read,
"Come and hear the Word of God."
In here, everybody is somebody
and Jesus Christ is Lord.

I parked my car and went inside,
surprised by what I had done.
Not missing a day at my church
unless something was really, wrong.

The sermon I heard blew my mind.
The spirit of fear God did not give.
If you pray every day,
it will change the way you live.

Once you are born again
fears power can be broken.
I clung to every word
the speaker had spoken.

This all can be done by faith
If you are determined to seek,
not just on Sundays,
but every day of the week.

I left there with the answer,
I knew I would return.
I found what I was looking for,
a place to grow and learn.

That Other Life

Everything was going wrong,
I thought I would lose my mind.
Storms of life when they come,
is never a convenient time.

I tried every trick in the book,
all of my life I was way off track.
deep in trouble,
with no more rabbits in my hat.

I knew if my life did not change,
I'd soon be buried in the ground.
I was slowly destroying myself,
I needed help to turn around.

I was somewhere I should not be,
with police all over the place.
Shots were fired, but none hit me.
I knew it was God's grace

When they took off the handcuffs,
they locked me up in jail.
I saw I had drifted far from God,
like a ship without a sail.

After I prayed I went to sleep,
believing God would work it out.
There I learned a valuable lesson,
do not go anywhere if I had doubt.

The next morning I was released
in an area I did not know.
I was broke, hungry and lost,
had no idea which way to go.

It was the most beautiful day.
I started singing my favorite song,
"This is the day The Lord has made,"
as I was walking along.

I felt a peace within my heart
It came with the morning dew.
I knew a change was coming
My other life was through.

Complete Control

I had so many problems
that would not go away.
I cried out to The Lord,
and I began to pray.

Dear God, "I do believe
Jesus Christ is your only son.
He gave his life to save my soul,
it was your will being done.

The blood he shed on the cross,
was to make me eternally free.
To conquer hell and death,
He went to Calvary.

Remove all doubts from my mind.
Please fill me with your spirit.
Take the sin, the guilt, the fears,
So when you speak I can hear it.

Help me do your will each day,
to make time to spend with you.
Be with me each step I take,
trusting you in all I do.

Help me build up my faith
so I will be able to stand.
When the strong winds blow,
my grip will be firm in your hand.

Let your blessing rain down on me,
in my heart, my mind, and soul.
I surrender all to you,
please take complete control.

No Limit

I drifted through my life
like a ship without a sail,
until one day, I stood shipwrecked.
Everything I tried had failed.

I had done so much wrong,
my life was full of confusion.
It was then I met the one
who gave me a solution.

He is the only way
my soul could be saved.
It was with the blood he shed
the way became paved.

I believe with all my heart
as I bow my head to pray,
confessing my sins and trusting Him
would change my life that day.

After I finished praying
I felt a difference inside.
Nothing I could see visibly,
yet I was full of confidence not pride.

Still I had to wonder
if this could really be
the God of all creation
having so much love for me.

His Word is showing me why
Jesus died and was raised,
to give me His salvation,
for this I give Him praise.

Now I know of his love.
God chose me to walk in it,
a love is everlasting
and without limit.

In Your Will

My life was going downhill,
I had no joy or peace.
I said to The Lord,
"Please help my unbelief."

Help me turn my life around,
help me trust you totally,
So I can learn your way,
to be the best that I can be.

Anything that hinders me,
please help me to remove.
In all I say and do,
I want you to approve.

Help me make the changes,
that will help me realize
how much you truly love me,
please open my spiritual eyes.

I cannot see into the future,
but in my heart I do believe
your plan for me is more wonderful,
than my mind can conceive.

Let your spirit work in me,
teach me to be quiet and still,
to seek, to learn every day, and
to walk in your will.

It Is Well

Something had to be done,
I did not know what to do.
Like a snow ball rolling down a hill
my troubles grew and grew.

I wanted my life to change,
but did not know where to begin.
I was at the end of myself,
I was tired of living in sin.

I decided to go to church,
hoping to find someone who would care,
but from the moment I walked in
all they did was whisper and stare.

So, I returned to my cardboard box,
my eyes filled with tears.
I was afraid to call on The Lord,
I Had not talked to Him in years.

I laid down and cried until
there were no tears to cry.
I thought maybe he would hear me,
no reason not to try.

Nedra Anthony ❧ 112

I said,
"Lord I hope you hear me.
I am sorry it took so long.
I want to return to your care,
only your strength makes me strong.

Open the doors to my heart and mind,
I need your help to start again.
I want my will to be your will,
led by your spirit from within.

I believe you hear, I am grateful,
although I lie here in the cold,
my heart knows
it is well with my soul.

Letting Go

In thought I went back to the day
when Jesus Christ and I first met.
It was a turning point in my life
I shall never forget.

I had failed at everything.
When he came into my life,
I went to my older brother
looking for some sound advice.

He said,
"One of the many reasons
Your life is way off track, is
You give your cares to The Lord,
then you keep taking them back.

He will help you let go,
you can leave your fears behind.
Seek Him and his kingdom first,
give Him control of your mind.

If you believe, he died for you,
that he rose from the dead,
for your soul's salvation,
His blood shed.

Nedra Anthony 🍃 *114*

The reason he became a man,
left His home above,
was so we could experience
the vastness of his love.

Because of God's great love,
the reason Jesus came.
Now you can let go of the past
that keeps on calling your name.

The Key

There are times I go to church,
with problems on my mind.
I even have the nerve to think
God will be glad I found the time.

I use my time working things out,
living life should not be hard.
It never even occurred to me
to cast my cares on The Lord.

I found it easy to believe,
all my dreams were out of range,
yet I found it hard to believe
if I wanted to, I could change.

I did not know where to start,
but I had to make a decision.
I knew I had to find a way,
out of my selfmade prison.

I thought back to times passed,
something Mama used to say,
"God always knows what you need,
so always remember to pray."

It seems she prayed all time,
the most prayerful person I've ever known.
She said, "The Lord has promised
He will never leave us alone."

You need His Word locked in your heart.
He will help you clearly see.
Faith is the substance of hope and
daily prayer is the key.

As A Servant

Almighty God knows everything
from the beginning to the end.
He knew man would disobey,
and would fall into sin.

Jesus came to prepare the way,
to give us a chance to choose,
to believe and trust in Him,
It is not wise if we refuse.

He said he is the only way
for man to receive salvation.
If we read and study his word
we will receive the revelation.

The Father gave all power to Jesus,
in His name, we can learn to trust.
Satan could not get Jesus to bow
therefore, he went to work on us.

Trust in God with every step you take.
Trust in the power of his might,
Satan hates us with a passion
when we let our light shine bright.

Keep thanking Him for allowing us
In Jesus name, to pray.
Many things are accomplished,
when we let Him lead the way.

Within us, a war is raging,
we must fight to have dominion.
When we have a right attitude
and not so free with our opinion.

When we begin to see
God's mercy and his grace,
that he sent his son to die
on the cross, taking my place.

A miracle occurred in my life
when I began to understand,
it was up to me to seek to find
how I fit into his plan.

When Steven was stoned, he stood
I know, He stands for me,
as a servant have I been good.

The Reason

On the first day of Christmas,
Jesus Christ, the savior was born
in a stable, then laid in a manger,
gathered straw kept Him warm.

A night star guided three wise men
as they traveled east,
to search for the new born king,
born to bring us peace.

He wants to live in your heart.
He wants you to be like Him,
to give the love he came to give,
and save you from being condemned.

This good news is for anyone
who is tired of living in strife.
A change will come through
Jesus Christ, a living sacrifice.

The world tries to knock you down,
but he won't let you fall.
Even when you cause your own trouble,
still he will hear when you call.

Nedra Anthony ❦ 120

So do not try to live without Him.
His love you would want to know.
Being a hearer and a doer
will help you learn and grow.

He had each one of us in mind,
even before, he created earth.
He is the reason for the season,
the time we celebrate His birth.

It's Already Mine

Jesus Christ died to save my soul,
So I had to make a decision
to live in bondage or be released
 from a selfmade prison.

Little did I know about God's love
or the joy His love could bring.
I am learning how to trust God
 who created everything.

I went through many changes.
My life was going downhill.
At the bottom, I met Jesus Christ,
where god's love was revealed.

All of my life God has been working
removing blinders from my mind,
opening my eyes so I could see
He was loving and kind.

It is because of His love
I do not do the things I used to do.
Knowing His love made life easier,
no matter what I had to go through.

I gave Him all of my burdens,
They were too heavy for me to bear.
He said to lay them at his feet,
and I must leave them there.

Now I am asking and seeking,
knowing one day, I will find
what God has for me
is already mine.

In The Morning

At first, I thought all would be well
when I received Jesus as my savior.
However, somewhere in my mind I thought
I was doing Him a favor.

I went to church three times a week,
to hear and learn His Word.
What I failed to understand,
I had not made Him my Lord.

I thought he ordered my steps,
although I seldom read His Word.
I heard it preached each Sunday,
not understanding what I heard.

He brought to mind how little time
I spent with Him in prayer,
but! Every time I called his name
He was always there.

His word has opened my eyes.
Each passing day I can see,
the plan God had from the beginning
was to save and set me free.

Nedra Anthony ❦ 124

Now that I know, I am learning
how to seek and find my way.
I know that I can talk to Christ,
anytime of the night or day.

Now I know I possess a love
nothing can ever destroy.
Weeping may keep me up all night,
but the morning comes with joy.

The Link

There is no bottom to God's love,
neither does it have a top.
It has no walls on either side.
His love will never stop.

God allowed His son to be crucified
and sins power was defeated.
After the price was paid in full,
Christ's mission was completed.

Jesus had total faith in His Father,
and after three nights and days
Jesus Christ, the Son of God,
rose up from the grave.

He brought with Him my redemption,
gave me the desire to do His will.
He gave me a measure of faith,
on which I was able to build.

I had to learn I could not conquer
anything I could not confront,
understanding who Jesus is
was my turning point.

Nedra Anthony ❦ 126

I had to look my fears in the face,
confront them eye to eye
knowing I could never let go of anything
if I kept refusing to try.

When I started looking at myself,
paying attention to how I was living,
I found I could depend on Jesus
and the love He was freely giving.

He paid the price on the cross,
shed His blood for my salvation.
Jesus Christ is the link between
God's love and His creation.

Don't Take God For Granted

I want to worship the Father in sprit.
His spirit will teach me truth.
He planned this day long ago,
even before, I entered my youth.

When I began to examine myself,
I gave myself the benefit of doubt.
I thought about all those times,
I knew it was God who worked things out.

I thought about how little time
my days were spent in prayer,
yet every time I called His name,
He was always there.

Then fear hit me like a flood,
my thoughts swept away.
The first thing that came to mind,
 was I never found the time to pray.

I did not even know the difference
between praising and worshiping God.
Most times when I did praise Him,
I was just grateful I had a job.

It seemed whenever I did pray
I always got what I asked,
He carried me all these years,
today I found it could not last

Now I am reaping the harvest,
of the fruitful seeds I planted.
Learning to walk by faith,
and not taking God for granted.

What Did Jesus Say?

I cannot make my brother change
if he chooses to be blind,
but I can tell Him what Jesus said
to help me change my mind.

I cannot choose the way
my sister wants to go,
but I can tell her what Jesus said
that helped me to learn and grow.

I cannot change the things
my husband decides to do,
but I can tell Him what I believe
that changed my point of view.

I cannot decide for my daughter
to give her life to Christ,
but she can see what He has done
that completely changed my life.

I cannot put a desire in their hearts
if they choose not to believe,
but they can see my confidence
that without a doubt I will succeed.

I cannot change their thinking
about the reason Jesus was sent,
but I can tell how in my heart, He gave me
the desire to repent.

I cannot refuse to tell them,
how He showered me with His love,
but I can tell them if they want to change,
they must be born from above.

I can tell them who Jesus really is,
and all he has done for me.
I can show by the life I live
that He has made me free.

I cannot be their Savior,
but I can tell them the way,
and before I speak I ask myself,
"What did Jesus say?"

The Truth

I traveled down many sinful roads,
desperately seeking a place
where I could find peace of mind,
no longer running to find a place to hide.

What my problem really was,
I did not have a clue.
I knew I needed help
but, I didn't know what to do.

I was tired of being tired.
Then I heard someone say,
"Jesus Christ is the answer
He is the light and He is the way.

Trust Him with all your heart,
give Him your every care.
when you need call Him,
He will be right there.

On my knees I said, "Lord, I believe.
Help me to find relief.
My life is a ball of confusion,
I have no joy or peace.

Nedra Anthony ❧ 132

Peace is what I asked for,
Peace is what he gave.
He gave me faith to believe
that my soul was saved.

Now I can receive all blessings
God has waiting for me.
I finally learned the truth,
The truth has made me free.

God's Way

I can hear a still small voice
when alone and set apart.
If I make time everyday
God will speak to my heart.

Walking in His strength and love,
is what helps me find my way.
My heart's desire is to know Him,
to walk closer to Him each day.

He has given my heart assurance,
as His wonders, I daily behold.
I praise Him with a thankful heart,
because He came just to save my soul.

He will help me love like Him,
as I daily, seek his face.
He gave His love to guide me,
preparing me to run life's race.

I learned how to pray in the spirit
So my soul cannot repel my prayers.
His still small voice speaks to me,
I am able hear it, I know he cares.

Prayer links me to the Father,
It is a must that I pray,
to gain the confidence and courage
to do God's will God's way.

His Dream

Martin had a dream,
gave his life to make it come true.
He was shot down in his prime,
trying to make life better for me and you.

He marched from city to city.
He marched to Washington D.C.
He was not looking for trouble,
all he wanted was for us to be free.

He fought for peace and harmony
between the white man and the black man.
He came under constant attack,
yet he was determined to stand.

He stood against the klu klux klan,
who thought blacks were less than men.
We must all come together in unity
or in the end they could win.

Where are we going wrong?
How can we turn our lives around?
Put down drugs, guns, and alcohol
and start using a mind that is sound.

Do not let Martin's death be for nothing,
on God's word he always stood.
If we do the same, lives will change to
 something beautiful and something good.

What was Martin's life really all about?
From Martin's life what can we glean?
The lesson is: one might take the life of a dreamer,
but one can never kill his dream.

Dr. Martin Luther King Jr.
January 15, 1929 – April 4, 1968

Endless Hope

God created me for better things,
so I allowed myself to succumb,
to the love I found when
I met God's only begotten Son.

He who came into this world,
so I could see the light.
I learned to walk by faith,
to never walk by sight.

All around was darkness.
My hope turned to despair.
All I was really looking for
was just someone to care.

Life's troubles were closing in.
I did not know which way was up.
I was told that Jesus loved me,
I could trust Him to fill my cup.

Now I am learning to trust Him
when things in life get hard.
I will do the best I can and
leave the rest up to The Lord.

Nedra Anthony ❦ *138*

I was getting nowhere without Him,
I had to give Him complete control.
He had given His life for me,
He came just to save my soul.

He will always be there for me,
even when I feel I cannot cope.
His Spirit will be my guide,
In Christ there is endless hope.

No Greater Love

I serve the Almighty God
who created heaven and earth.
He placed a star in the eastern sky
to announce my Savior's birth.

He was born to pay the price
for the sin sick souls of man.
He chose to give His life
according to His Father's plan.

He who is the Son of God,
many wanted to see Him dead.
It was on the cross at Calvary
where His blood was shed.

He knew the road He had to travel.
He knew how His journey would end.
He would die and rise again,
to make man free from sin.

Then early on the third day,
the full price had been paid.
The stone was rolled away,
then from death, He was raised.

Nedra Anthony ☙ 140

His life and death changed the world.
All men could choose to be free.
Once I had made my choice,
I learned to walk in victory.

His Word showed me how to live
by God's will from above.
Jesus conquered hell and death,
there can be no greater Love.

A Job Well Done

For years I was searching
with a desire to understand,
why the God of all creation,
fit me into His master plan.

Everything that He is
within and of Himself,
is selfsufficient,
He does not need my help.

He made a road through my wilderness,
which only He could do,
He sent His Son to the cross
to give His life for me and you.

When he took control
of my life, he chose to give,
He began a work in me
completely changing the way I live.

He showed me His unlimited love,
on which I learned to rely.
He showed how much He loved me
when as a man He chose to die.

Nedra Anthony ❦ 142

My renewed mind leads me in battle
trusting each word, He has spoken.
So, when the battle is over
sins power would be broken.

It is necessary I keep fighting,
not letting sin get the upper hand
blocking each flaming dart sin shoots at me,
I am learning how to stand.

So, on the day I stand before Him,
when my final day has come.
I pray that He will say to me,
"My child, a job well done."

www.ingramcontent.com/pod-product-compliance
Lightning Source LLC
Chambersburg PA
CBHW020909090426
42736CB00008B/547